Harry Saves The Ocean!

n.g.k.

Illustrated by Janelle Dimmett

N.G.K. — To Kate, Happy 40th Birthday!
SF — For my beautiful girls, Scarlett, Sienna and Sylva.

First published worldwide on 3rd August 2019.

Story by N.G.K. (and Sylva Fae)
Illustrations by Janelle Dimmett
Text and illustrations copyright © 2019 N.G.K.
Written in the Cabin.

Thanks to Millie Slavidou.

Also dedicated to anyone who spends any of their time working towards cleaning up the oceans.

ISBN:
Paperback - 978-1-9160811-0-9
Hardback - 978-1-9160811-1-6
89378290KC

All rights reserved, including the right of reproduction in whole or in any form. Work may Not be used without the publisher's permission.

FIRST EDITION

On the crest of a wave and the wisp of the wind,

Harry The Happy Mouse was packing his things.

The family were excited, "Let's laugh and let's cheer,
Not far to go now, the beach is quite near."

"The coast is in sight, it's just down the track."
"Hooray!" shout the family "It's nice to be back!"

The children smiled at the sight of the sea,
While Harry and Katie unpacked with great glee.

The happy mice raced to their holiday house,
It was small and cosy, just right for a mouse.

Harry set off on his sandy beach walk,
"I wonder who I'll find for a lovely beach talk?"

The sunlight danced on the clear blue sea,
The waves hit the beach, so wild and free.

"Help me! Please help me!" called a voice from the sea.
"There's a bag on my head, and I just can't get free."

Along the whale's back, the mouse swiftly sped.
And pulled off the bag from the mighty whale's head.

"Oh dear!" said Harry, "This seems strange to me,
What on earth is a bag doing in the sea?"

"It's dumped," said the Whale. "The fish are so sad,
Thinking and dreaming of the home they once had.

The ocean is full of rubbish you see,
And that is so bad for them and for me."

"Your bags and your bottles, your bucket and spade...
The trouble with plastics, they don't biodegrade."

"Biodegrade?" said Harry, "Explain this to me,
What does it mean for you and the sea?"

"Well, paper and cardboard and food rot away,
But plastic won't rot so it's here to stay."

"It ends up in the ocean, and clogs up the sea,
And that is a problem for you and for me."

"Oh dear!" said Harry, "That'll never do!
But if we all join together, we can help you!

I'm just a small mouse but I've got a big plan,
We will clean up the sea, I know that we can!"

"Excuse me, seagulls, can you help me?"
Harry explained how much help they could be.

"It's a big job for one but if we all lend a hand,
We'll soon make a difference to the sea and the sand."

"Hello Mrs. Turtle can you help me?
It'll be a great job when we've cleaned up the sea!

It's a big job for one but if we all lend a hand,
We'll soon make a difference
                              to the sea and the sand."

"Hello there, Mr Puffin, and Pelican too!
I've got a great plan for me and for you!

It's a big job for one but if we all lend a hand,
We'll soon make a difference to the sea and the sand."

"The plastic is harmful to you and to me,
I'm sure that the crabs can help clean up the sea?

It's a big job for one but if we all lend a hand,
We'll soon make a difference
                        to the sea and the sand."

Harry and Katie, the little mice too,
Joined up with the rest of the beach clean-up crew!

"Come on!" said Harry, "We can see this through!"
And every creature had something to do.

They picked up the bottles, the packets and bags,
They collected the cartons and packaging rags.

Harry was happy and shouted to all,
"Ok everyone, now follow my call!

Put the plastics in red, the glass goes in green.
Wow! Look what we've done! This beach is so clean!

By stopping the plastic getting into the sea,
We're saving the ocean for you and for me!"

Harry looked happy, "What a great day!
All of the beaches should look this way.

Spread word to your friends, birds of the sea,
Let's make our beaches and seas, plastic free!"

The messenger seagulls set off on their quest,
Spreading the word from the east to the west.

"Clear up the plastic, it's dangerous, you see.
It's better for all who live in the sea."

Harry waded out to explain what he'd done.
"Your beach is now clean, go swim and have fun!"

"Thank you, kind mouse!" said the dolphins and whales.
They saluted the helpers with waves of their tails.

"It was a big job for one but we all lent a hand,
We soon made a difference to the sea and the sand."

On the crest of a wave, and the wisp of the wind,

Harry, and his helpers, had done wonderful things.

Other books in the bestselling Harry The Happy Mouse Series:

Book 1 — Harry's Lovely Spring Day

Book 2 — Harry The Happy Mouse

Book 3 — Harry's Spooky Surprise

Book 4 — Harry The Christmas Mouse

Please visit:
www.harrythehappymouse.com

www.ingramcontent.com/pod-product-compliance
Ingram Content Group UK Ltd.
Pitfield, Milton Keynes, MK11 3LW, UK
UKHW052121230426
12049UKWH00009BA/142

9 781916 081116